ELI MANNING
and the
New York Giants

SUPER BOWL XLVI

by Michael Sandler

Consultant: Charlie Zegers
Football Expert and Writer

BEARPORT
PUBLISHING

New York, New York

Credits

Cover and Title Page, © Jamie Squire/Getty Images; 4, © Anthony J. Causi/Icon SMI/Newscom; 5, © Lionel Hahn/ABACAUSA.COM/Newscom; 6, © Chad Ryan/ Cal Sport Media/Newscom; 7, © Bob Rosato/Sports Illustrated/Getty Images; 9, © Bob Leverone/Sporting News/Getty Images; 10, © Rich Kane/Icon SMI/Newscom; 11, © Norm Hall/Getty Images; 12, © AP Photo/Matt Ludtke; 13, © Icon Sports Media/Newscom; 14, © Rick Stewart/Getty Images; 15, © Jonathan Ernst/Reuters/ Newscom; 16, © Jeff Gross/Getty Images; 17, © Aaron Suozzi/ABACAUSA.COM/ Newscom; 19, © Rob Carr/Getty Images; 20, © AP Photo/Kevin Terrell; 21, © John G. Mabanglo/EPA /Landov; 22L, © Anthony J. Causi/Icon SMI/Newscom; 22R, © Wesley Hitt/Getty Images; 22Background, © Icon Sports Media/Newscom.

Publisher: Kenn Goin
Senior Editor: Lisa Wiseman
Creative Director: Spencer Brinker
Design: Debrah Kaiser
Photo Researcher: James O'Connor

Library of Congress Cataloging-in-Publication Data

Sandler, Michael.
  Eli Manning and the New York Giants : super bowl XLVI / by Michael Sandler.
      p. cm.
  Includes bibliographical references and index.
  ISBN 978-1-61772-578-4 (library binding) — ISBN 1-61772-578-1 (library binding)
  1. Manning, Eli, 1981—Juvenile literature. 2. Football players—United States—
Biography—Juvenile literature. 3. New York Giants (Football team) —Juvenile
literature. I. Title.
  GV839.M2877S26 2013
  796.332092—dc23
  (B)
                                        2012016966

For more information, write to Bearport Publishing Company, Inc., 45 West 21st Street, Suite 3B, New York, New York 10010. Printed in the United States of America.

10 9 8 7 6 5 4 3 2 1

★ Contents ★

Miracle Man

In 2012, the New England Patriots had a 17–15 lead over the New York Giants with less than four minutes left to play in Super Bowl XLVI (46). The Giants needed to score if they hoped to win this game. However, quarterback Eli Manning and his team had a long way to go. The Giants were about to start a **drive** from their own 12-yard (11-m) line.

Four years earlier, Eli had pulled off the impossible in a similar situation against the Patriots. He led an end-of-game drive to deliver Super Bowl XLII's (42) winning touchdown. The Giants' **upset** win had shocked the Patriots and the world. Could Eli deliver one more miracle for his team?

Eli Manning (#10) calls a play during Super Bowl XLVI (46).

Eli looks to pass during
Super Bowl XLVI (46).

In 2012, the Giants were trying for the
fourth Super Bowl win in team history. In
addition to Super Bowl XLII (42), the Giants,
led by quarterback Phil Simms, defeated
the Denver Broncos, 39–20, in 1987's Super
Bowl XXI (21). Then in 1991, running back Ottis
Anderson starred in New York's 20–19 victory
over the Buffalo Bills in Super Bowl XXV (25).

Football Family

As a child, Eli Manning grew up surrounded by the game of football. His father, Archie Manning, had been a New Orleans Saints quarterback. His older brothers, Cooper and Peyton, played football in high school. Peyton even went on to become a superstar at the University of Tennessee. He then became one of the NFL's great quarterbacks, winning a Super Bowl with the Indianapolis Colts in 2007.

Eli shared his family's love for the game. He learned to throw the football like his brothers and father. At both Isidore Newman High School in Louisiana and the University of Mississippi, he earned honors for his passing.

Indianapolis Colts quarterback Peyton Manning gets ready to throw the ball.

Eli in action during a game for the University of Mississippi

Eli set 45 different passing records at the University of Mississippi. In his senior year, most people considered him the country's best college quarterback.

Super Bowl Superstar

After Eli graduated from college, the San Diego Chargers chose him first in the 2004 NFL **draft**. However, he was traded to the Giants before the start of the season. During his first few years on the team, he gradually developed into a top NFL quarterback. In both the 2005–2006 and 2006–2007 seasons, he helped the Giants reach the **playoffs**. His greatest success, however, came the following year.

Although the Giants finished with just a 10–6 record in the 2007–2008 regular season, they won three tough **road games** in the playoffs to reach Super Bowl XLII (42). Meanwhile, their opponent, the New England Patriots, had gone **undefeated** all season. They were also led by three-time Super-Bowl-winning quarterback Tom Brady. Amazingly, Eli outplayed Tom to lead the Giants to a shocking 17–14 Super Bowl win!

In Super Bowl XLII (42), Eli completed 19 of 34 passes for 255 yards (233 m) and two touchdowns for the win.

Eli (#10) celebrates with teammate Brandon Jacobs (#27) after the Giants defeated the New England Patriots in Super Bowl XLII (42).

2011

Eli and the Giants followed up their Super Bowl victory by winning their **division** the next season. The following two seasons, however, the team played poorly, missing the playoffs both years. Then in the 2011–2012 season, with just a 9–7 regular-season record, New York returned to **postseason** play. However, with their poor record, their fans wondered if the team even had a chance of making it to the Super Bowl.

Though their record didn't show it, the Giants had played brilliantly at times. They had overcome some serious injuries, and Eli led New York to six come-from-behind victories. He and Giants coach Tom Coughlin didn't care what anyone else thought. They believed their team could return to the Super Bowl.

Eli (left) talks to Coach Coughlin (right) on the sidelines during a 2011 game.

Hakeem Nicks (#88) catches the winning touchdown pass from Eli in the Giants 31–27 comeback win against the Arizona Cardinals on October 2, 2011.

In 2011, Eli set an NFL record with 15 fourth-quarter touchdown passes, many during the Giants' six comeback wins.

Three Stops to the Super Bowl

The road to the Super Bowl began in Atlanta. In New York's first playoff game, the Giants' defense smothered the Atlanta Falcons for an easy 24–2 win. Next, the Giants traveled to Wisconsin to face Aaron Rodgers and the Green Bay Packers. Once again, the Giants were fantastic, defeating the Packers in a 37–20 victory.

The victory against the Packers sent New York into the **NFC Championship Game** against the San Francisco 49ers. Tied 17–17 after **regulation**, the Giants won the game on Lawrence Tynes's overtime field goal. Eli and Coach Coughlin were right. The Giants were headed to Super Bowl XLVI (46)!

Giants Corey Webster (top left) and Michael Boley (bottom left) knock down Green Bay Packers quarterback Aaron Rodgers (right).

Eli completed 32 passes for 316 yards (289 m) and 2 touchdowns in the win against San Francisco.

Four years earlier, on the way to Super Bowl XLII (42), New York had won the NFC Championship Game in the same way that they did in 2012. Lawrence Tynes had kicked an overtime field goal in a 23–20 victory over Green Bay.

Rematch

The Giants' win set up a Super Bowl **rematch**. Once again, New York would be facing Tom Brady and the New England Patriots. As in Super Bowl XLII (42), the Patriots would be the favorites. Including the playoffs, the Patriots had a 16–3 record and had won their last ten games.

It was also the fifth Super Bowl trip for Tom Brady and his coach Bill Belichick, and they especially wanted to win. After all, four years earlier New York had spoiled New England's perfect season.

Tom Brady (#12) gets his
team ready for a play.

Tom Brady in action during a game in 2011

The Giants had won three out of four previous Super Bowl games. Their only loss came in 2001's Super Bowl XXXV (35) matchup against the Baltimore Ravens.

The Game Begins

The Giants were also determined to win and they proved this early on. On New England's first **offensive** play, New York **defensive end** Justin Tuck charged forward as Tom Brady dropped back to throw. To avoid a **sack**, Tom tossed away the ball. The officials **penalized** Tom for intentional grounding. The Giants were awarded a **safety** and an early 2–0 lead.

New York's offense was as fierce as its defense. Eli used six different **receivers** to bring the Giants downfield for a touchdown. Now New York led 9–0. The Patriots, however, fought back. Tom's accurate passing helped New England to a field goal, a touchdown, and a 10–9 halftime lead. Then an early third-quarter touchdown extended the Patriots' lead to 17–9.

Eli set an NFL record by completing his first nine passes in Super Bowl XLVI (46), including this touchdown pass to Victor Cruz (right).

16

Depending on his position on the field, a quarterback usually can't just throw the ball away to avoid a sack. He must throw it toward a receiver or the play is considered intentional grounding. On the Justin Tuck play, there were no receivers near the place where Tom's pass landed. Since Tom would have been sacked in the **end zone**, a safety resulted.

Justin Tuck (#91) forces Tom Brady (#12) to throw the ball away.

A Magic Pass for Mario

For the Giants to win, Eli would now need to direct another New York comeback. He led New York on two third-quarter scoring drives. Both, however, ended in field goals.

New England held on to a 17–15 lead as the clock ticked down in the fourth quarter. Then, with only 3 minutes and 46 seconds left to play, the Giants began a final drive from their own 12-yard (11-m) line.

On the first play of the drive, Eli spotted receiver Mario Manningham running far downfield by the left sideline. Two New England defenders draped themselves over Mario, but Eli's pass—a perfect spiral— landed directly in his outstretched hands. Suddenly the Giants were at midfield. Four passes later, New York had moved all the way to the Patriots' 6-yard (5-m) line with just over a minute left to play.

New England coach Bill Belichick claimed that Mario's feet were out of bounds on his catch. The referees looked at the replay but ruled that Mario had clearly caught the ball in bounds.

"Eli put a great ball out there," said Mario Manningham, shown here catching the ball. "After I caught it I think the whole team figured we were going to win this."

Champions Again

Now New York could run down the clock and then try for a field goal as time ran out. If the kick was good, the Giants would win. Eli had put New England into a desperate situation so the Patriots made a huge gamble. They decided to let New York score. With one minute and four seconds to play, Giants running back Ahmad Bradshaw fell into the end zone for a touchdown—untouched by New England defenders.

This strange play gave New York a 21–17 lead, but it also allowed the Patriots to get the ball back. Now they would have a chance to score a touchdown before time ran out. In the end, the gamble failed. The Giants' defense proved too strong, and the Patriots failed to score. Eli and the Giants had defeated New England again. They were the Super Bowl champions once more.

Ahmad Bradshaw (right) falls into the end zone for the game's winning touchdown.

Eli celebrates the Giants' victory.

After the game, Eli was named Most Valuable Player (MVP) of Super Bowl XLVI (46). He had also been named MVP of Super Bowl XLII (42).

★ Key Players ★

There were other key players on the New York Giants who helped win Super Bowl XLVI (46). Here are two of them.

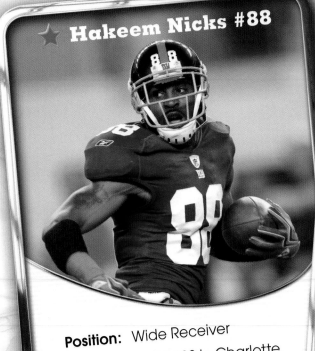

★ Hakeem Nicks #88

Position: Wide Receiver

Born: 1/14/1988 in Charlotte, North Carolina

Height: 6' 1" (1.85 m)

Weight: 208 pounds (94 kg)

Key Plays: Caught ten passes for 109 yards (100 m)

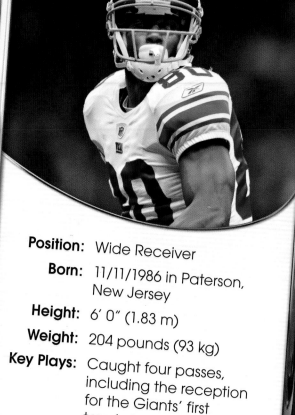

★ Victor Cruz #80

Position: Wide Receiver

Born: 11/11/1986 in Paterson, New Jersey

Height: 6' 0" (1.83 m)

Weight: 204 pounds (93 kg)

Key Plays: Caught four passes, including the reception for the Giants' first touchdown

defensive end (di-FEN-siv END) a player whose main jobs are to stop the run and put pressure on the quarterback

division (di-VIZH-uhn) teams that are grouped together in the NFL and that compete against one another for a playoff spot

draft (DRAFT) an event in which NFL teams choose college players to be on their teams

drive (DRIVE) a series of plays that begin when a team gets the ball; the drive ends when the team with the ball either scores or gives up the ball to the other team

end zone (END ZOHN) an area at either end of a football field where touchdowns are scored

NFC Championship Game (EN EFF SEE CHAM-pee-uhn-*ship* GAYM) a playoff game that decides which National Football Conference (NFC) team will go to the Super Bowl

offensive (aw-FEN-siv) having to do with the players on a team who are responsible for scoring points

penalized (PEE-nuh-*lized*) given a punishment or penalty by the referees for breaking one of the game's rules

playoffs (PLAY-awfs) final games to decide which teams will play in a championship

postseason (POHST-see-zuhn) after the regular season; the playoffs

receivers (ri-SEE-vurz) players whose job it is to catch passes

regulation (reg-yuh-LAY-shuhn) the length of an NFL game, or 60 minutes; if a game is tied at the end of regulation play, an extra period called overtime is added

rematch (REE-mach) a second contest between two teams that have already played before

road games (ROHD GAYMZ) games that are played on the opposing team's home field

sack (SAK) when a quarterback is tackled behind the line of scrimmage

safety (SAYF-tee) a play in which an offensive player is tackled in his own end zone, resulting in two points for the defensive team

undefeated (uhn-duh-FEET-id) not having lost a single game

upset (UHP-set) when the team expected to lose beats the team expected to win

Bibliography

The New York Times

Sports Illustrated

NFL.com

Read More

MacRae, Sloan. *The New York Giants.* New York: PowerKids Press (2011).

Sandler, Michael. *Eli Manning and the New York Giants: Super Bowl XLII (Super Bowl Superstars).* New York: Bearport (2009).

Sandler, Michael. *Tom Brady and the New England Patriots: Super Bowl XXXVIII (Super Bowl Superstars).* New York: Bearport (2008).

Learn More Online

To learn more about Eli Manning, the New York Giants, and the Super Bowl, visit **www.bearportpublishing.com/SuperBowlSuperstars**

Index